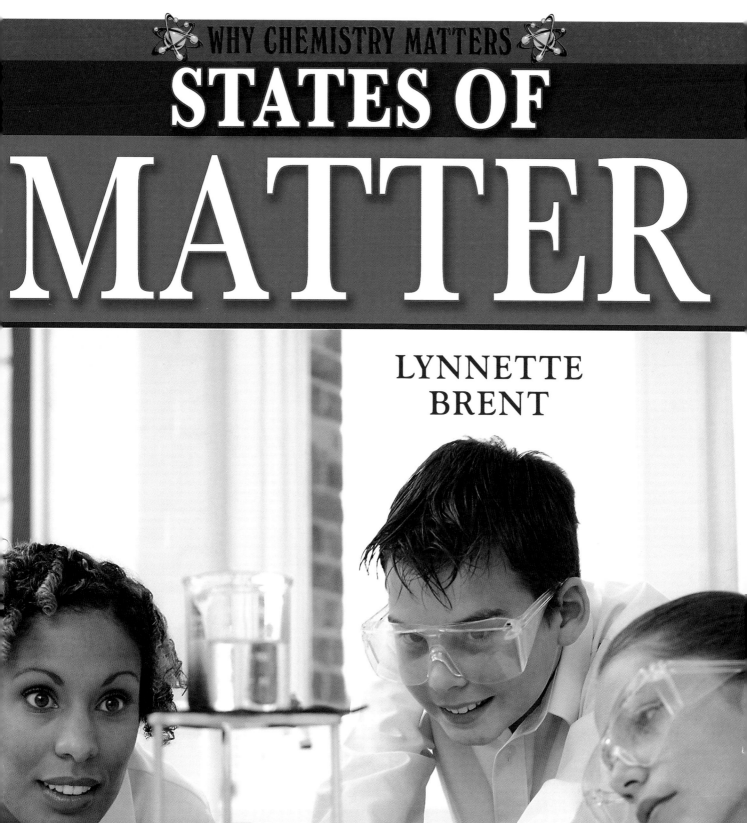

WHY CHEMISTRY MATTERS

STATES OF

MATTER

LYNNETTE BRENT

Crabtree Publishing Company

www.crabtreebooks.com

Crabtree Publishing Company

www.crabtreebooks.com

Author: Lynnette Brent
Coordinating editor: Chester Fisher
Series editor: Scholastic Ventures
Editor: Adrianna Morganelli
Copy editors: Molly Aloian, Reagan Miller
Proofreader: Crystal Sikkens
Project editor: Robert Walker
Production coordinator: Katherine Kantor
Font management: Mike Golka
Prepress technicians: Samara Parent,
    Katherine Kantor, Ken Wright
Project manager: Santosh Vasudevan (Q2AMEDIA)
Art direction: Dibakar Acharjee (Q2AMEDIA)
Cover design: Ranjan Singh (Q2AMEDIA)
Design: Neha Gupta (Q2AMEDIA)
Photo research: Anju Pathak (Q2AMEDIA)

Photographs:

Cover: Sebastian Duda/Shutterstock; Title page:
Inspirestock/Jupiter Images; P4: Gelpi/Shutterstock;
P6: NASA; P7: Pidjoe/Istockphoto; P9: Bakalusha/
Shutterstock; P10: Ljupco Smokovski/Fotolia;
P11: Robert Shantz/Alamy; P12: 4grapher/
BigStockPhoto; P13: NASA; P14: Govorov
Pavel/Shutterstock; P15: Boris Ryaposov/
Shutterstock (top); P15: Brian Chase/Shutterstock
(bottom); P16: Dusan Zidar/Shutterstock; P17:
Rtimages/Dreamstime (left); P17: Phototake
Inc/Alamy (right); P18: Polka Dot Images/Jupiter
Images; P19: Magnascan/BigStockPhoto; P20:
Gene Chutka/Istockphoto; P21: Jason Maehl/
Shutterstock; P22: Lawrence Cruciana/
Shutterstock; P23: NASA; P24: Viktor Kitaykin/
Istockphoto; P25: H D Connelly/Shutterstock;
P26: Raja Rc/Dreamstime; P27: Altiso/Shutterstock;
P29: Olga Kushcheva/Shutterstock

Illustrations:

Q2A Media Art Bank: Cover (insets), P5, 8, 19, 23, 28

Library and Archives Canada Cataloguing in Publication

Brent, Lynnette, 1974-
    States of matter / Lynnette Brent.

(Why chemistry matters)
Includes index.
ISBN 978-0-7787-4244-9 (bound).--ISBN 978-0-7787-4251-7 (pbk.)

    1. Change of state (Physics)--Juvenile literature. 2. Matter--
Properties--Juvenile literature. 3. Chemistry--Juvenile literature.
I. Title. II. Series.

QC301.W43 2008   j530.4   C2008-904141-0

Library of Congress Cataloging-in-Publication Data

Brent, Lynnette, 1974-
    States of matter / Lynnette Brent.
        p. cm. -- (Why chemistry matters)
    Includes index.
    ISBN-13: 978-0-7787-4251-7 (pbk. : alk. paper)
    ISBN-10: 0-7787-4251-2 (pbk. : alk. paper)
    ISBN-13: 978-0-7787-4244-9 (reinforced library binding : alk. paper)
    ISBN-10: 0-7787-4244-X (reinforced library binding : alk. paper)
    1. Change of state (Physics)--Juvenile literature. 2. Matter--Properties--
Juvenile literature. 3. Chemistry--Juvenile literature. I. Title. II. Series.

QC301.B74 2009
530.4--dc22
                                                    2008028897

Crabtree Publishing Company

www.crabtreebooks.com   1-800-387-7650

Printed in the USA/012010/CG20091228

Published in Canada
Crabtree Publishing
616 Welland Ave.
St. Catharines, ON
L2M 5V6

Published in the United States
Crabtree Publishing
PMB 59051
350 Fifth Avenue, 59th Floor
New York, New York 10118

Published in the United Kingdom
Crabtree Publishing
Maritime House
Basin Road North, Hove
BN41 1WR

Published in Australia
Crabtree Publishing
386 Mt. Alexander Rd.
Ascot Vale (Melbourne)
VIC 3032

Contents

The Stuff Around You

Take a look around. Everything around you is made of **matter**. Matter is anything that takes up space. There are three main forms of matter. Matter can be a **solid**, like ice. Matter can be a **liquid**, like water. Matter can also be a **gas**, like **steam**. Matter can change forms. If you **freeze** water, for example, it becomes a solid—ice. Do you want the water back? Turn up the heat!

Matter has to be made of something. Everything in the universe is made of **elements**. Elements cannot be broken down into simpler substances. Gold is an element, for example. You can heat gold to very high temperatures, and it will **melt**. No matter what you do to it, it will still be gold. Water, on the other hand, is not an element.

You probably know that water has a formula: H_2O. The H stands for hydrogen, and the O stands for oxygen. These are the elements that come together to make water.

Everything in the universe is made of matter— even you!

That is not quite the whole story, though. Elements themselves are made of tiny particles called **atoms**. The element gold is made of gold atoms. Water is hydrogen and oxygen atoms. Atoms are the building blocks of matter. Atoms are too small to see with the naked eye. **Molecules** are groups of atoms. In water, a group of two hydrogen atoms and one oxygen atom is a molecule.

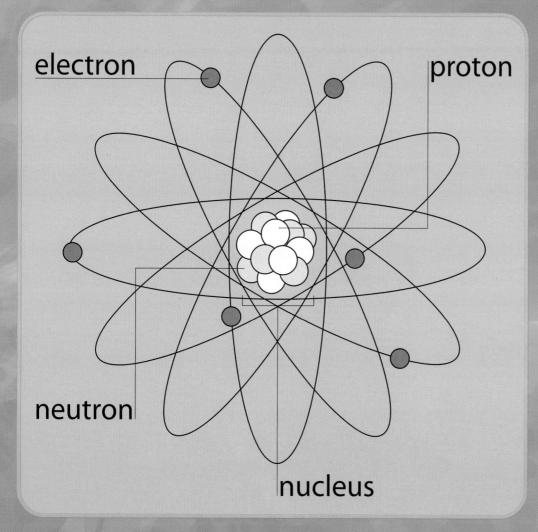

electron

proton

neutron

nucleus

Particles called protons, electrons, and neutrons are the parts of an atom.

What is Inside an Atom?

*An atom is a tiny particle that has three parts: **protons**, **neutrons**, and **electrons**. Protons and neutrons are inside the core, or **nucleus**, of an atom. The electrons circle around the outside of the nucleus. Each element has a different number of protons. An atom of the element hydrogen always has one proton. At atom of gold has 79 protons.*

Measuring Matter

If you have stepped on a scale, you have measured matter. Why else might you measure matter? Imagine if you put the wrong amount of flour in a cookie recipe!

The amount of matter in an object is its **mass**. In other words, mass is how much matter an object contains. Mass is usually measured in ounces (oz.) or grams (g).

Volume is the amount of space an object takes up. When you cook, you might add one cup of milk to your pancake batter. One cup is the volume of milk—that is how much space the milk takes up.

Why can this astronaut float? The Moon has less gravity than Earth. This means that an astronaut weighs less on the Moon.

Imagine holding a metal block in one hand and a wooden block in another. They are exactly the same size, but they do not have the same mass. Why not? The metal block has a greater **density**. Density measures how heavy something is for its size. If the atoms in material are packed closely together, the density is greater than in a material in which the atoms are far apart. You can figure out an object's density by dividing its mass by its volume. Density is the reason that rubber ducks float on top of the bath water. The ducks have a lower density than water, so they float. Objects that are denser than water—like rocks—will sink.

Mass, Weight and the Moon

Stepping on a scale measures your **weight**. *Mass is the amount of matter in an object. Mass never changes. Weight measures the effect that gravity has on an object. Say you weigh 93 pounds (42 kg) on Earth. The Moon has 1/6 of the gravity of Earth. Less gravity means less weight. On the Moon, you would weigh only 15.4 pounds (7 kg)!*

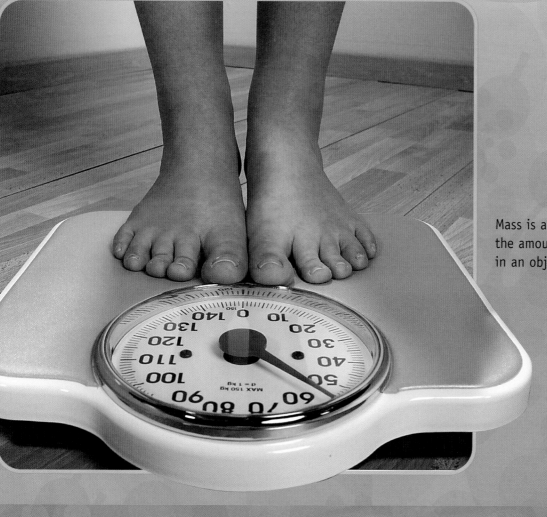

Mass is a measure of the amount of matter in an object.

What are Solids?

Many materials are solids at room temperature, from French fries to your favorite shoes. A solid can hold its own shape. If you poured water from a tall glass to a short glass, the water's shape would change. But a solid ice cube will keep its shape whether it is in a glass, an ice cube tray, or on a plate in the freezer. The container just has to be in a cold place. A diamond will always look like a diamond. You could grind a diamond up into a powder, but if you looked at that powder under a microscope, you would still see solid pieces of diamond.

The particles in solids are arranged in tight, repeating patterns. They are "stuck," so solids keep their shapes.

Why does a solid hold its shape so well? You already know that all matter is made of tiny particles called atoms or molecules. In a liquid or gas, there is space between those particles. The particles can move around to other positions. But in a solid, the materials are packed very closely together. Because the molecules are "stuck," they cannot move much. That keeps them close together in the form of a solid.

Your shoes and French fries are not elements! They are made of many different elements. Some elements are solids at room temperature. Concrete is a solid strong enough to hold heavy trucks on top of it. What other solids are important in your life?

Solid as a Rock

Many elements are solids in their most common forms. Metals such as iron, copper, gold, and silver are all elements that are solid at room temperature. These metals will not melt into liquids unless heated to very hot temperatures. Gold, for example, will only melt at temperatures above 1,947 degrees Fahrenheit (1,064 degrees Celsius). As soon as it cools, it becomes solid again.

All solids, like these wooden blocks, have a fixed shape and volume.

What are Liquids?

Your blood is a liquid. So is the water you drink. Liquids have something in common with solids. Liquids, like solids, take up a certain amount of space. If you pour water from a small bowl into a big bowl, the water will not grow to fill up the space.

Unlike solids, though, liquids do not have a set shape. When you have milk in a measuring cup and then pour it into a bowl, the amount of milk is the same. Its shape changes, though. Solids are made of particles that are packed close together.

Because the particles cannot move, the shape of the solid is "set." The particles in liquids are different—they have a little more "wiggle room." That freedom lets liquids flow and change shape.

Liquids have no fixed shape. They take on the shape of whatever container they are in.

Solids are often measured by mass. Liquids are measured by volume instead. Soda cans usually hold 355 mL (12 oz.) of liquid. Milk cartons can hold 3.8 L (one gallon) of milk. Ounces and gallons are both measures of volume. We also measure volume in liters. A gallon of thick, heavy cream might have more mass than a gallon of water, but they both take up the same amount of space.

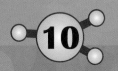

Walking on Water

*A sticky force holds liquid particles together. That force makes water act like it is covered with a stretchy "skin." This stretchy surface is called **surface tension**. Surface tension makes water bead up into drops instead of spreading out. Have you ever heard of water striders? These bugs walk on water because of the water's surface tension.*

Insects called water striders can walk on the surface of water because of surface tension, a sticky force that holds liquid particles together.

Gases and Plasma

It sounds like a riddle: It is all around you, but you cannot see it. It surrounds Earth and keeps it warm, yet it is not a blanket. What is it? Gas! Do not confuse the word gas with the liquid you put into the family car. A gas is the third main state of matter. The **atmosphere** is a big layer of gas that blankets the entire Earth. Carbon dioxide is a gas that comes from us when we breathe. Plants use this gas and give off another gas: oxygen.

Neon signs get their glow from the neon gas inside them.

Fourth State?

*One other **state** exists; but it is not often seen on Earth! **Plasma** is an electrically charged state of matter. It forms when a gas gets so hot that electrons break away from its atoms. Plasma forms in the hot gases of the Sun. On Earth, plasma is created inside lighting. Plasma is also artificially created inside nuclear power plants.*

Just like liquids and solids, the properties of gases depend on the way that atoms and molecules are arranged inside the material. In solids, the particles are close together. In liquids, the particles like to stick together, but they can spread out a bit. Gases can really spread out because the atoms and molecules are bouncing around and moving apart.

Gases can fill any container, from a balloon to a room. The gases will spread out in any size or shape.

A liquid sticks to the bottom of the bowl because of gravity. But gases are light enough that they can spread upward. Can you imagine if you blew up a balloon and the air inside stuck just to the bottom of the balloon? The air fills up the balloon and expands it in every direction.

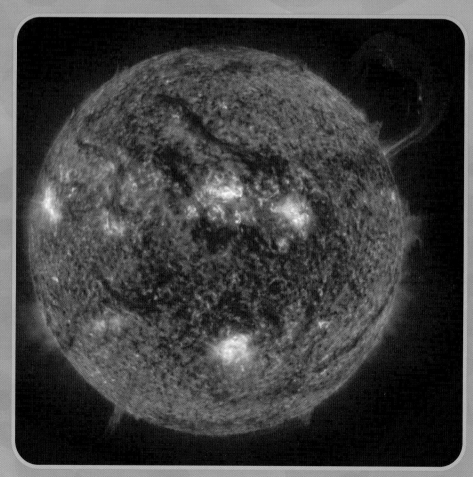

On the Sun, gases get so hot that they become electrically charged, forming a fourth state of matter called plasma.

Solids to Liquids

Did you ever leave a box of solid crayons on the dashboard of the car? What happened to them? Most likely, they melted. Solid matter became liquid matter—it had a change of state. This change of state happened because of a change in temperature. The sun coming through the windshield made the waxy crayons melt.

Many solids, when heated, will melt to become a liquid. Some solids melt at lower temperatures than others do. The temperature at which a solid substance melts is called its **melting point**. When a liquid cools, it may freeze. This temperature is the **freezing point**.

How does heat make a substance change states? Heat is energy. When heat energy is added to a solid, the particles in the solid have a bit more room to move and can start to spread out. With enough heat, the particles can move around enough to flow as liquid.

Lakes can harden into ice rinks when outdoor temperatures drop below the freezing point of water.

Liquid Mercury

Most metals, such as nickel, copper, and zinc, are solids at room temperature. One exception is the element mercury. Mercury is a toxic, silvery liquid named after Earth's planetary neighbor Mercury. The element mercury is often found inside glass thermometers, barometers, and other scientific equipment. Temperatures must drop to nearly –38°F (–39°C) before mercury hardens into a solid!

Glass thermometers contain mercury, a silvery metal that is liquid at room temperature

For any substance, the melting point of its solid state is the same as the freezing point of its liquid state. In other words, the melting point of ice is 32°F (0°C). The freezing point of water is also 32°F (0°C). Different substances, though, have different melting and freezing points. While ice melts at 32°F (0°C), the metal silver will not melt until temperatures hit 1762°F (961°C).

When chocolate is heated past its melting point, it changes from a solid state to a liquid state.

Liquids to Gases

When you **boil** water on the stove, the liquid becomes warmer. If you add enough heat, the water boils. The water becomes steam, which spreads invisibly all around the kitchen. Liquid to gas is a change of state for matter. When heat energy is added to a liquid, the particles in the liquid move farther and faster. Eventually, the liquid takes on enough heat energy to boil. The temperature at which a liquid boils is its **boiling point**. When a gas cools below the boiling point, it **condenses**, or changes into a liquid.

Sometimes, liquids become gases at temperatures lower than the boiling point. Maybe you have noticed that on a sunny day, a puddle of water on the sidewalk will slowly shrink and disappear. The water is not really vanishing. It is changing from liquid to gas, even though the outdoor temperature remains below water's boiling point (212°F or 100°C). You might not be able to see the gas, but it is there.

When water vapor comes in contact with a cool drink, the vapor condenses to form drops of liquid.

As the sun warms the puddle, particles at the surface of the water become energized. Some of the particles manage to escape into the air, turning into a type of gas called **water vapor**. This is **evaporation**. Evaporation occurs when liquid changes to a gas at temperatures below the boiling point.

Skipping a Step

*Some substances change directly from solids to gases, skipping the liquid state in between. This is **sublimation**. Solid carbon dioxide is commonly known as dry ice. When it is heated, dry ice turns directly from a frozen solid into carbon dioxide gas. If the carbon dioxide gas cools again, it turns back into a solid.*

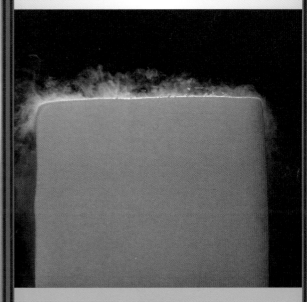

Dry ice is known for sublimation, turning directly from solid to gas without passing through a liquid state.

Evaporation occurs when some surface water molecules escape into the air, turning from liquid to gas.

Under Pressure

Pressure can also affect states of matter. Pressure is the amount of force pushing down on a particular area. If you stood with one book on your head, you could feel the book's pressure. What if you stood with a pile of books on your head? The pressure would be greater, with more mass focused on the same area.

The atmosphere is a layer of gases that exerts pressure on Earth. If you were to dive deep below the surface of an ocean, you could feel the pressure of the water pushing against you. When pressure changes, a substance's melting and boiling points change, too. As you know, water boils at 212 °F (100 °C) at normal air pressure. What would happen if you tried to boil water on top of a mountain? On top of a mountain, thousands of feet above sea level, the air exerts less pressure. With less pressure to overcome, particles in the water can break free of their liquid bonds more easily. Water would boil at a lower temperature.

Scuba divers have to wear special clothing and use special equipment to dive where the water pressures are great.

At high **altitudes**, liquid water changes to gas at temperatures below 212 °F (100 °C). In other words, boiling point goes down when pressure goes down, and boiling point goes up when pressure goes up. Pressure affects melting points in the same way.

The boiling point of water can change when the pressure changes. Someone cooking in the mountains will have boiling water more quickly.

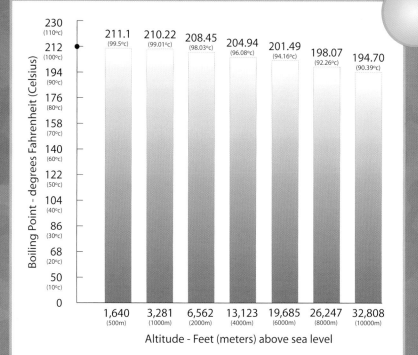

Boiling Over

This graph shows the relationship between altitude (height above sea level) and the boiling point of water.

Spotlight on Water

Water exists in all three states of matter—solid, liquid, and gas. And it exists in these forms in temperatures you would regularly find on Earth.

Water covers most of Earth in the form of rivers, lakes, and oceans. Water's solid state, ice, is a common sight on winter days and inside your freezer all year long. You make water's gaseous state, steam, every time you boil water. Steam is invisible. When you see white clouds above a pot of boiling water, you are witnessing water droplets condensing back into a liquid as they cool in the air.

Water vapor is a gaseous form of water that is usually present in the air. **Humidity** is the amount of water vapor in the air. On humid days, there is a lot of water vapor in the air. On very dry days, the air holds little water vapor. When water vapor condenses into a liquid, it forms the water droplets that make up rain or fog.

Water is the most plentiful — and most important — liquid on Earth.

Geysers spew hot liquid water droplets and steam into the air.

Water in the Body

All living things need water to survive. The human body is about 65 percent water. Every cell in your body needs water to function properly. Water helps keep your body temperature stable. When you get too hot, you sweat. As the water in the sweat evaporates from the surface of your skin, it takes excess heat with it, cooling you off.

Life on Earth depends on the water cycle. The Sun heats up Earth's water and causes evaporation. Then the water vapor gets cold, turning into clouds. When clouds get heavy, water comes back to Earth as rain, hail, sleet, or snow. This precipitation ends up back in our river, lakes, and oceans. The water you drank today may have cycled for millions of years!

Spotlight on Air

An empty box is never really empty. It is filled with the special mixture of gases we call air. Earth is surrounded by a protective envelope of gases called the atmosphere. The lower part of the atmosphere is referred to as "air."

The atmosphere is a colorless, odorless, tasteless group of gases. One gas in the air is oxygen. Life on Earth could not exist without oxygen. Animals breathe oxygen to survive. Luckily, there is enough oxygen in the air for everyone.

Air also contains some water, in the form of water vapor, as well as fine dust and pollutants. The atmosphere keeps us warm and shields us from harmful radiation from space. High in the sky, far from the surface of Earth, the atmosphere gets thinner. As it thins, it exerts less pressure onto the surfaces around it.

The air we breathe is mostly nitrogen and oxygen. When we go underwater, the gases are scarce—so divers take those gases with them!

The air surrounding Earth is sometimes called the "third atmosphere." In the history of Earth, the air has changed. At first, our Earth was surrounded by helium and hydrogen. Then about 4 billion years ago, eruptions from volcanoes began to change the atmosphere. Today, the atmosphere has much more oxygen than it did long ago.

The elements that make up the air are always in gas form at temperatures found on Earth. If you could cool air to -328°F (-200°C), it would condense to form a blue-colored liquid.

The gases of Earth's atmosphere protect us from harmful radiation from space.

Gases in the Air We Breathe

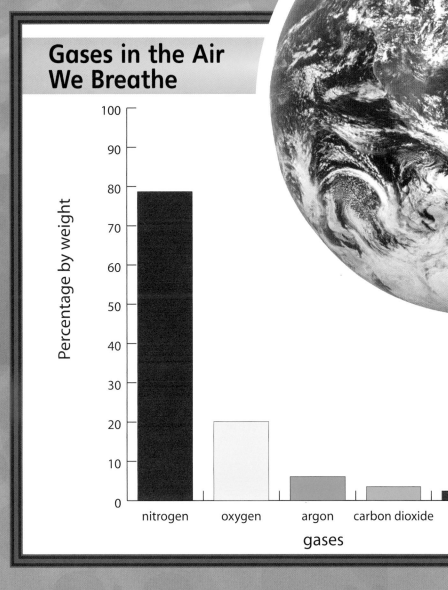

Percentage by weight

| 100 |
| 90 |
| 80 |
| 70 |
| 60 |
| 50 |
| 40 |
| 30 |
| 20 |
| 10 |
| 0 |

nitrogen   oxygen   argon   carbon dioxide   other

gases

Elasticity

Different materials have their own properties. Scientists can use these properties to describe and classify materials. What properties can be used to classify materials? Another property used to describe solids is **elasticity**. Elasticity is the ability of a solid to recover its size and shape after it has been stretched or squeezed.

Rubber bands, bouncing balls, and bubble gum are highly elastic. You can stretch them and smash them, and they will not break. Solids that have low elasticity are more rigid and brittle. Porcelain and glass have low elasticity. If you drop a coffee mug or a light bulb, it will probably break. Its inability to bounce back into shape means that the material has low elasticity.

Objects made of porcelain have low elasticity. This means they break easily and will not reform their shapes.

24

Some very thick liquids have elasticity as well. With these fluids, you could apply very quick pressure that could change the liquid's form. Take the pressure away, and the fluid would return to its normal shape.

Elastic solids can be stretched and squeezed without breaking them.

Hands On: Toy Maker

Make your own bouncing ball, an example of an elastic solid.

Supplies:
Borax powder (found in the laundry section of the store)
Cornstarch
White school glue
Warm water
Measuring spoons
Plastic cups and spoon

1. In one cup, mix 2 tablespoons (30 mL) of water with ½ teaspoon (2.5 mL) borax. Stir until the borax dissolves.

2. In another cup, pour 1 tablespoon (15 mL) of glue. Add ½ teaspoon (2.5 mL) of the borax solution you just made into the glue. Then add 1 tablespoon (15 mL) of cornstarch. Do not stir the mixture yet!

3. Let the ingredients sit for 15 seconds. Then, stir them together with a plastic spoon. Once the mixture gets too hard to stir, remove it from the cup and knead it with your hands.

4. As you knead the mixture, it will solidify into a bouncy ball. Bounce it! How elastic is your ball?

More Properties

Some solids, like clay, can easily be formed into other shapes without breaking. Solids like these are malleable. **Malleability** is the ability of a solid to be molded without breaking. Many metals are malleable. Silver can be hammered to form cups and jewelry. The opposite of malleable is brittle. Brittle substances can crack or break under pressure.

Solids can also vary in their **hardness**. Hardness is the ability to resist scratching. Hard objects, such as steel knives, are difficult to scratch. Soft objects, like chalk, are easy to scratch. Diamonds are the hardest naturally occurring substance known. Diamonds can scratch all other minerals.

Liquids have their own unique properties. A liquid's ability to resist flowing is called its **viscosity**. Liquids with low viscosity flow easily when you pour them. Thick, sticky liquids have high viscosities. This means they flow very slowly. Viscosity changes with temperature and pressure. Syrup, for example, has more viscosity cold than when it is warm.

Honey is a viscous liquid. It is thick and it flows very slowly.

How Hard?

A substance's hardness is measured against the Mohs Scale. The scale rates the hardness of minerals, from 1 (very soft) to 10 (very hard). To find the hardness of a material, look to see what it can scratch and what can scratch it. For example, if a material is scratched by apatite but not by fluorite, then its hardness on the Mohs Scale is between 4 and 5. What would the hardness be of a material that can scratch quarts but not topaz?

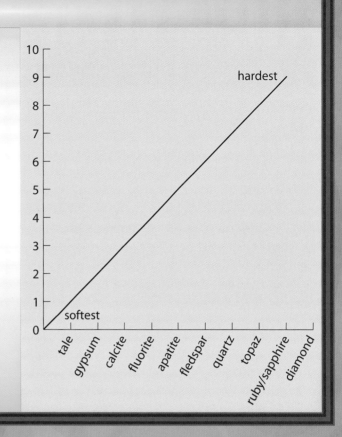

Diamonds are the hardest material known.
They can scratch all other gems and minerals.

The Fifth State

You already know about liquids, solids, gases, and plasma. But there is a fifth kind of matter, one that is very rare and actually very new. Two scientists, Eric Cornell and Carl Weiman, created Bose-Einstein Condensates in 1995. So why isn't this matter called Cornell-Weiman condensate? Because two other scientists, Albert Einstein and Satyendra Bose, predicted this state of matter in 1920. They did not have the equipment that they needed to create it.

Plasma is created by applying heat to atoms so that they become very excited. Bose-Einstein Condensates are the opposite. The atoms are very unexcited because they are at extremely cold temperatures. To understand this matter, first you have to understand condensation. When gas comes together, the molecules slow down and then begin to collect. When they collect, a liquid forms. The same thing happens when you boil water with a lid on top of the pot. The water cools and becomes a liquid—the liquid is condensation.

On the Kelvin scale, atoms stop moving at absolute zero. Even the farthest reaches of space are 3 degrees.

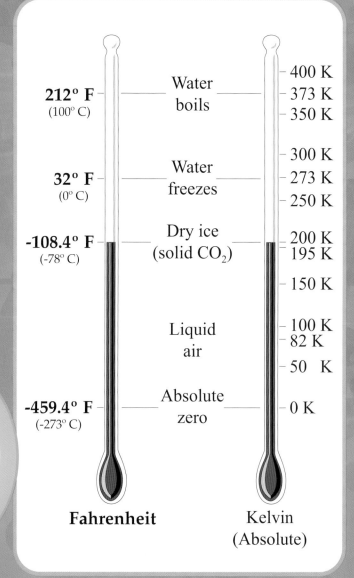

212° F
(100° C) — Water boils — 400 K / 373 K / 350 K

— 300 K

32° F
(0° C) — Water freezes — 273 K / 250 K

-108.4° F
(-78° C) — Dry ice (solid CO_2) — 200 K / 195 K

— 150 K

Liquid air — 100 K / 82 K / 50 K

-459.4° F
(-273° C) — Absolute zero — 0 K

Fahrenheit

Kelvin (Absolute)

The Future of Bose-Einstein Condensation

Bose-Einstein Condensates are very fragile, and physicists can only make a few million atoms of them at a time. Physicists are still figuring out ways to make more of this state of matter.

Bose-Einstein Condensates act in a very similar way to laser light. Scientists think that, someday, this special state of matter can be used for making very sensitive measurement instruments.

When water boils, the gases form condensation on the lid of the pot. The condensation is water.

Bose-Einstein Condensation happens only at extremely low temperatures. At zero Kelvin, all motion stops. Atoms do not move, so there is no motion at all. Scientists have found a way to get the temperature extremely close to absolute zero. At this temperature, Cornell and Weiman used the element rubidium to create a condensate. When the temperature gets that low, the atoms start clumping together. This "super atom" is a Bose-Einstein Condensate. Only a few elements can create this.

Glossary

altitude The height of a point above sea level

atmosphere Gases that surround and protect Earth

atom Microscopic particle that makes up all matter

boil To change from a liquid to a gas

boiling point The temperature at which a substance changes from a liquid to a gas

condense To change from a gas into a liquid

density The concentration of particles within a substance; density is equal to mass divided by volume

elasticity The ability of a material to recover its size and shape after being squeezed or stretched

electron Negatively charged particle that orbits the nucleus of an atom

element A substance that cannot be broken down into a simpler substance by chemical means

evaporation To change from a liquid to a gas at a temperature below the boiling point

freeze To change from a liquid to a solid

freezing point The temperature at which a liquid changes to a solid

gas State of matter with no fixed shape and no fixed volume

hardness The ability to resist scratching

humidity The amount of water vapor in the air

liquid A form of matter with a fixed volume, but no fixed shape

malleability The ability of a solid to be molded without breaking

mass The amount of matter in an object, often measured in ounces (oz.) or grams (g)

matter Anything that occupies space

melt Changed from a solid to a liquid

melting point The temperature at which a solid changes to a liquid

molecule Two or more linked atoms

neutron Uncharged particle in the nucleus of an atom

nucleus The core of an atom, which contains neutrons and protons

plasma A fourth state of matter formed when gases get so hot that they become electrically charged

pressure The amount of force pushing down on a surface

proton Positively charged particle in the nucleus of an atom

solid State of matter with a fixed shape and a fixed volume

steam A gaseous form of water

sublimation To change from a solid to a gas without passing through the liquid phase

surface tension Sticky force that makes liquids behave as if they were covered by a stretchy "skin"

state The physical form of a substance

viscosity The ability of a liquid to resist flowing

volume The amount of space that an object takes up

water vapor A gaseous form of water

weight The force of gravity acting on a body of matter

Index

Web Finder

http://www.chem4kids.com

http://www.exploratorium.edu/ronh/weight

http://www.rsc.org/chemsoc/visualelements/pages/periodic_table.html

http://www.reactivereports.com/index.html

http://www.spartechsoftware.com/reeko

http://www.webelements.com

32

Printed in the U.S.A.